Prai

"In *Divine Trust*, Dr. Nancy powerfully guides us to experience a deep sense of safety and love that is fundamental to living our best lives. This profound state will transform your world and strengthen your connection to the Divine. As you use the techniques in this book, you'll experience greater heart-opening and trust in the universe. Let it lift, carry, and nourish every aspect of your being."

—Marci Shimoff,
#1 *New York Times* best-selling author *of Happy for No Reason*, *Love for No Reason*, and *Chicken Soup for the Woman's Soul*, featured teacher in *The Secret*, founder of *Your Year of Miracles*

"*Divine Trust* is an essential state of mind and the entry point into your very own relationship with the Divine. Our own embodiment of this state is our true liberation. Dr. Wiley captures with clarity the exact steps needed to achieve this foundational state. Once this connection is made, your life will be forever changed. This is a brilliant must-read user's manual for humanity."

—Dr. Sue Morter,
founder Morter Institute for Bio-Energetics, author of *The Energy Codes*, Developer of BodyAwake Yoga, Host of *Healing Matrix* for Gaia TV, Co-Host of *Your Year of Miracles*

"I love Dr. Wiley's book! It is so needed at a time when there is so much uncertainty. As she says in the book, 'This is more than just a book, it's a map to true happiness'. This is true, and even more, it is a constant reminder to trust the process of life as long as we stay in true connection with the Divine."

—Lisa Garr,
host of *The Aware Show*,
author of *Becoming Aware*

"*Divine Trust* is a must-read for anyone who has ever suffered, whether from outside events or internal worry and stress. Dr. Nancy Wiley shares her journey and teaches us with clarity and ease how to quiet our chaotic inner chatter and develop our own direct connection with Source, our touchstone within."

—Suzanne Lawlor M.A.,
Master Coach, *Your Year of Miracles*

"*Divine Trust* by Dr. Nancy Wiley shows us all a way home and an end to all suffering. In this compelling book, Dr. Nancy weaves together some of life's most profound truths and shows us all a clear path to greater happiness and joy. It all begins by opening our hearts, learning to let go, and trusting in the universe. Filled with inspiration and proven techniques, Dr. Nancy's book shows us how to release our fears and move into a state of grace and greater inner peace. Readers will emerge with a deep understanding of the divine perfection that is always supporting and guiding us. This is a must-read for anyone wanting to experience greater levels of happiness, joy, and harmony with all that is."

—Judi Miller,
author of *Perfect: A Path to Love, Forgiveness and Transformation*

DIVINE
TRUST

DIVINE TRUST

A Practical Guide to
End Your Suffering and
Find Your Way Home

DR. NANCY WILEY

About the Front Cover

This picture was taken one foggy morning
as the sun was rising.
The sunbeams were radiating like the arms
of *God* reaching out to embrace me.
The setting was so surreal that I felt like this
was a direct message
of confirmation from the *Divine* that I was
indeed on the right path
to bring the knowledge of *Divine Trust* to you!
The idea of putting it on the front cover
of my book did not dawn on me
until my Miracle sister, Mary Forehand,
powerfully suggested this.

Divine Trust
A Practical Guide to End Your Suffering and Find Your Way Home

Copyright © 2022 Dr. Nancy Wiley

info@TrustTheDivine.com
TrustTheDivine.com

Editing and Proofreading: Angela Valentine, Mary Forehand and Judy Finkell
Cover Designer: Pagatana Design Service—pagatana.com
Book Interior and E-book Designer: Amit Dey—amitdey2528@gmail.com
Publishing Consultant: Geoff Affleck, AuthorPreneur Publishing Inc.—geoffaffleck.com

ISBN: 978-1-7375434-0-4 (Paperback)
ISBN: 978-1-7375434-1-1 (eBook)

Library of Congress Number: 2021918720

OCC011020 **BODY, MIND & SPIRIT** / Healing / Prayer & Spiritual
OCC019000 **BODY, MIND & SPIRIT** / Inspiration & Personal Growth
SEL016000 **SELF-HELP** / Personal Growth / Happiness

Dedication

I dedicate this book to the
students and teachers of
Marjory Stoneman Douglas High School and the
Parkland and Coral Springs communities.
May you Trust in *The Divine* once again.

Bonus Meditation

Download your companion supportive gifts before you start reading.

In order for you to get the absolute most out of this book, I have created companion audios to accompany you as you practice the processes in *Divine Trust*. You will be entering into states that do not use your mind for navigation. Rather, you will be using your own consciousness in the *Present Moment*. It is extremely helpful to listen to the recordings to get into these new states of *Being* instead of reading them from the book. It is my intention that these audios fill your life with sublime and profound *Divine Trust*.

You will receive 8 audios:

1. Chapter 3 Explanation: How to Enter into the State of *Being* of *Divine Trust*

2. Chapter 3 Process/Meditation

3. Chapter 4 Meditation: The Advanced Method

4. Chapter 5 Explanation/Process: How to Reinforce *Divine Trust*

5. Chapter 6 Explanation/Process: How to Work with *Divine Trust* to End Suffering

**Download the free audios at
trustthedivine.us
or scan the QR code.**

Names for *The Divine*

*F*or clarity and distinction, names for *The Divine* are written in an italic calligraphy script font throughout this book and include the following:

All

All That Is

All That Is Energy

Being, Divine Being, Beingness

Bigger Than Me, Bigger Than Me State Of Being, Bliss

Consciousness, Pure Consciousness

Divine, The Divine, Divinity, Divine Trust

Divine Presence

Energy, Divine Energy, Energy Source

Essence, Divine Essence

God

Higher Self

I Am

It, Itself

Light, The Brotherhood of Light

Love

Oneness, The One

Presence, Present Moment

Sea Of Awareness

Source

Spirit

This

Unity, Unified Field, Unified Field Consciousness

You And Me

Prologue

As this was going to publication, I received this message from *Source/God*:

"We bless you with this knowledge. We bless you with this shining *Light* that can help you *all* assimilate these Truths!

You all carry this knowledge inside you. It is now the time for you to awaken to your own Truth!

This is the Evolution that *must* and will take place.

It is up to each of you to accept, embrace, and Trust, or not. But eventually, you will Know! Now *is the time*!

Now is your time to shine!"

Contents

Foreword

What an extraordinary time to be living now! Chances are that if you're attracted to this book, you feel like you're a part of the massive shift in human consciousness that is taking place—a transformation to greater wholeness, well-being, and harmony.

Albert Einstein once said, "The most important question a person can ask is, 'Is the Universe a friendly place?'" How we answer that question will guide the quality of our life and our shift in consciousness.

In these unprecedented times, Trusting that the Universe is a benevolent and friendly place is a truly revolutionary perspective.

As we face a global pandemic, worldwide shutdowns, environmental challenges, and civil unrest here in 2021, we're presented with many reasons to be worried and anxious about the future.

The lesson from an old Cherokee parable can serve us well during these times. A Cherokee grandfather shares with his grandson that each of us has two wolves fighting inside of us. One wolf is full of anger, regret, self-pity, and resentment. The other wolf is full of love, generosity, truth, compassion, and faith.

When the grandson asks the grandfather which wolf will win the fight, the grandfather replies, "The one you feed."

Every day, as we're bombarded with reasons to be afraid, we each have an important choice to make about which thoughts and feelings we'll feed. Will we choose fear? Or will we choose Trust? In *Divine Trust,* Dr. Nancy Wiley shares her profound perspective and wisdom for choosing Trust.

I've had the great privilege of being a mentor to Nancy for the past seven years, as she's been a member of my program, *Your Year of Miracles,* which supports people to live more miraculous lives. A miracle is defined as "a surprise and welcome event that can't be explained by science and that's considered to be Divine grace." We can't create miracles, but we can create the conditions for miracles. One important key to doing that is choosing to Trust that there is Divine perfection in every situation, as the Universe is *on our side.* I've been inspired by witnessing Nancy choose Trust again and again, and it's been a joy to observe how that has helped her experience more miracles in her life.

In *Divine Trust,* Nancy provides a step-by-step guide for how to fully embrace the path of Trust. She offers us powerful ways to Trust that we live in a benevolent Universe—even when appearances tell us otherwise. Nancy shows us how this remarkable choice can transform our lives on every level, rippling out to transform all of humanity.

I've witnessed Nancy choosing Trust in the most challenging situations. As an orthodontist working in Parkland, Florida, she was inspired to share this knowledge in the aftermath of the violence at Marjory Stoneman Douglas High School. She saw the impact of this violent event on the community and longed to be of service. Rather than operating from fear, Nancy chose to Trust. She turned her pain into fuel for change and for sharing this message of Trust with the world.

Nancy has shared with the *Your Year of Miracles* group that Trust is her *way home*. She committedly applies what she teaches in this book, and she states that no matter what's happening or how "bad" her day seems, as soon as she shifts into a profound state of Trust, every negative impression dissolves. Nancy not only has an innate understanding of Trust, but she also embodies it.

By practicing what she teaches in this book, you, too, will be able to reach this sublime state of being. It's as if an outstretched hand is lifting you, enlightening you, giving you hope, and clearly illuminating the way out of suffering.

Nancy provides a steadfast guide to the brave path of Trust. Living in this way will open you to miracles beyond your greatest imagination, and you'll be helping to create a world where we all rise in love, freedom, and unlimited possibility together.

— Marci Shimoff,
#1 *New York Times* best-selling author of
Happy for No Reason, Love for No Reason,
and *Chicken Soup for the Woman's Soul,*
featured teacher in *The Secret,* and
founder of *Your Year of Miracles*

Introduction

The Grace of *Divine Trust*:
The Key to Ending Suffering and
the Key to the Deepest
Relationship with *Source*

*B*old claims, but true. I challenge you to allow me to prove these claims. Reading this book will only take about two hours. Isn't learning the key to ending suffering and gaining an intimate relationship with *The Divine* worth that small investment? Take your time; digest this truth. Let it nourish you. Let it transform you!

I have traveled in spiritual circles for forty-three years as of this writing. Those four-plus decades of study have taught me this truth: the way to have a deep abiding Trust in *Source/The Universe/God*, or any other name you give *The Divine*, is to know *It*! The way to know *It* is to sit with *It*, commune with *It*, talk to *It*, and let *It* reveal *Its* characteristics. The more you do this, the more *It* will reveal *Its* properties, *Its* unchanging, constant traits. These traits are fundamental and reproducible.

When I sit in this *Energy*, I find *It* Loving, Gentle, Generous, Warm, Nurturing, Caring, Benevolent, Dependable, Intelligent, Sentient, and Always There. *It* is inside of me, outside of me, in everything—including all humans and all things, animate and inanimate—and existing everywhere. How I see the *Universe* has actually evolved for me over time, because I sit in *Its* presence so much. I see and experience us all as *One*. Every one of us can know the same truths: this vast *Sea Of Awareness* is unassailable, constant, true, and comforting.

When you see the world from this vantage point, there is no such thing as a "bad" day. Whenever I start to get worked up about something (which I still do), I hand the dense, contracted thought or emotion over to this *Energy*; and when I commune with *It*, the emotion or the state of *Being* just melts into the same light, expanded vibration as *Source*, and it is transformed!

This is *Divine Trust*.

In this book, I will be your guide, and I will teach you how *you* can also do this. My confidence and my experience will illuminate your way through this discovery. You will learn that the state of *Divine Trust* starts by opening your heart and being willing to allow a new state of *Being*.

> **In your hands, you currently hold the key to unlock the end of suffering. More than just a book, this is a map to true happiness.**

I invite you to join me in this journey and discovery of *the way home*!

CHAPTER 1

Working Model of Existence

W hat you are about to read is not immediately apparent to everyone. It may not yet be time for all humans to embrace these truths. However, if you find yourself reading these words, and they seem to resonate with something deep inside, then you are ready to know these truths. If what you are about to read does not seem possible, then put this book away until It calls to you, for one day It will! Then you will know it is your time to be enlightened.

Everything starts with an understanding and acceptance of how we came into *Being* and of certain fundamental concepts of how our world works. In the beginning, there was one *Energy*. *It* knew how amazing *It* was, but wanted to experience *Itself* more fully. To do so, *It* chose to expand into matter. The beginning of all matter could very well be explained by something similar to the Big Bang theory. I have come to know that this action of *Source* becoming matter was, in fact, how all matter was originally created.

After expanding into matter, *It* could now experience *Itself* more fully through *Itself* as everything that exists. And yet, though everything that exists may appear to be composed of separate elements, all matter still remains in *It*s original essence as only one *Energy*—a vast ocean of loving *Presence*. In time, the human form was also created from this matter, evolved, and perfected. In human form, this *Energy* could be both conscious of *Itself* and conscious of *Itself* as *The Divine Presence*.

However, our human design is such that somewhere during the process of being born, we undergo amnesia to the understanding that we are, in fact, the very embodiment of *The Divine Itself*. The longing and the urge to understand who we are and find the way home is common among *all* human beings and is the purpose and the way *Presence/Source/God* comes to know *Itself*.

Before our soul took a physical body, *It* chose prime lessons *It* wanted to have as challenges/opportunities. Some of these challenges come in the form of core wounds. All humans experience core wounds, which might occur simply from a rebuke of a parent, sibling, or relative, or which might be deeply tragic, such as experiencing abuse or witnessing a heinous crime. Generally, the more shocking or profound the core wound, the bigger/stronger the *Spirit* is that chose this core wound for the lessons *It* would provide. These core wounds, as part of the human condition, bring about suffering.

Fortunately, once we understand our design, our soul will wake up to the truth of *Its Being*. This truth is that our *Being* is both body and *Divine Presence*. The full comprehension of this understanding (our soul's AHA moment) most often occurs gradually, but can sometimes happen suddenly. Understanding this design and being awakened to the fact that we are *Divine* is— what I like to call—a **Snap Back**. Our souls are *awakened*, i.e., *snapped back*, to the full knowledge that our design is so profound that we ourselves are *Divine*. Recognition and acceptance of this fact completely changes our life!

This AHA moment comes when we know ourselves to be here in a body, but are also conscious of ourselves as this vast *Sea Of Awareness*. This is why we incarnate— to know ourselves as the amazing *Being* and *Presence* of *All That Is*, as *Source*! In fact, we are a walking body with *God* looking directly through our eyes. *God* is using our hands, our feet, our mouth, and our actions to experience *Itself*! Remember that *God* wants to know *Itself* and just how expansive and amazing *It* actually is! The **Snap Back** to this understanding is why the design is the way it is. This is the fundamental truth!

If, and when, we come to understand the working model of our true design and can come to Trust it, then we have a **Snap Back** to our original *Essence*, knowing without a doubt that we *are* the *Divine Presence*! This is the very purpose of incarnating, so that *God* can know *Its* magnificence! Once this happens, we can say we are enlightened. Furthermore, if we are able to retain this certainty of the truth of our *being home*, then this is the end of suffering. This is when we are truly *home*. This is the evolution of mankind!

> **This is our Purpose! Now we are Awake! Now we are Free!**

CHAPTER 2

Foundation of *Divine Trust*

*H*ow does one come to know and Trust *Source*? Usually, there is some sort of inner guidance, or we are able to be still long enough to hear/feel this urging. It has always been with us, as it is our purpose for being born. Sometimes, we are lucky enough to be in the right place at the right time to hear someone who has already found the way home. Or maybe we are given a book, or something crosses our path that captures our attention. It is at this point that the seed we call 'seeking' emerges. Thus begins our insatiable, lifelong search for more and more information that touches our core.

My own seeking began at the age of sixteen when I received a book from an open-minded friend. He thought I might like the book, *The Power of Your Subconscious Mind*, by Dr. Joseph Murphy, which greatly shifted my perception of reality and became one of my favorite books.

Almost simultaneously, my mother developed an interest in Transcendental Meditation (TM) and wanted to learn the technique. When I was seventeen, she took me with her to learn TM. She had heard it would help with stress. She needed it for herself and thought it would be good for me, too, as I was so intense and driven. Although I was able to reach deep relaxation through TM, it ultimately did not teach me how to navigate through all of my life experiences, as you will learn to do in this book.

During those formative years, I also had dear friends about 25 years older than I who had immigrated to the United States from India. Somehow, they knew that I was a seeker. This couple helped me foster my seeker thirst by encouraging me and giving me books to read, which I devoured. One of the most influential was, and remains, Paramahansa Yogananda's *Autobiography of a Yogi*.

Since I was raised Catholic, I went to Catholic School from Kindergarten through Grade 4. Then we moved to a city where Interfaith Sunday or Saturday services were encouraged. We went to church almost every week. During my collegiate sophomore year, I took a *Sociology of Religion* course that pushed the premise that there was no *God* and that the major religions were developed to control or manipulate the masses. This eye-opening revelation was like having the rug pulled out from under my feet! The result was that I felt incredibly empty and betrayed for years.

However, something I will never forget happened while I was a dental student at Columbia University. The medical and dental students study together for the first three years. Sitting high up in a semi-circular amphitheater lecture hall, we were learning about immune responses, different types of T-cells, lymphocytes and leukocytes, and how the body responds to eradicate any impending virus or bacteria. Suddenly, an inner flash of *Light* occurred. I experienced a *huge* **Snap Back** moment. I *knew* instantly, and have never doubted since:

> The human body and the design of these most miraculous processes could *only* be designed by a *Being* so Intelligent, Benevolent, and Loving that this design had to have been created by a *Divine Being*!

From that moment on, I knew, to my core, that there was an *Energy* that designed us. I knew, unquestionably, that *Divine Being*, that *Energy*, was and is Benevolent and wants us to live in health. This was a pivotal point for me, because it was a visceral knowing that there is an amazing *Energy* that is constantly conspiring for our greatest good! Being certain of this conviction that behind the veil was a big *Presence*, I felt compelled to know more. However, my demanding dental school schedule would not allow much time to continue being a seeker. Nevertheless, my thirst and internal drive remained.

During the span of years after my seeker AHA awakening moment described above, numerous synchronistic and psychic events deeply touched my life and joined together, like the pieces of a puzzle, to bring me to this moment of writing this book and sharing this profound, life-changing truth. Once a human *Being* awakens to this knowing, they may start to listen more to their own intuition, or to guidance from outside *Divine Beings*, or, perhaps, to their own Higher Self.

Being trained in the medical field develops the left brain and teaches you to see what is concrete. Generally, most branches of science tend to lead away from intuition or right-brain thinking and the ability to personally experience *The Divine*. Scientific thinking almost forces the right brain to close off. Despite this, my right brain refused to be silenced.

A few years later, while I was still at Columbia University, but now studying orthodontics, my mother found out she had stage III breast cancer. The tumor was the size of a grapefruit, and even though she had annual mammograms, it had been completely missed. A physician's assistant first saw the puckering in her left breast during a routine pre-op medical clearance exam for a minor knee arthroscopy.

My mother was then scheduled to have a radical mastectomy followed by chemotherapy. Her surgery was scheduled for a Monday. I came home to be with her the weekend before and planned to stay for a few days. The Friday before surgery, my mother asked me to come with her to a Catholic Church Mass in the foothills of Maryland. The Mass was set for sunset and was held in a small chapel with side walls that were almost entirely windows. As the sun was setting with exquisite beauty, I reflected on the incredible magnificence of this backdrop. It was almost as if we were being embraced by the spectacular colors of the setting sun, visible on three sides of this mountain perch.

At the end of the Mass, the priest announced that he would do a *laying-on-of-hands* for anyone who desired it. My mother asked me to wait in line with her. When her turn came, the priest asked her to identify her malady. She told him, and he took her head in both of his hands. He held her head for at least ten minutes. Then the priest whispered, "you are healed."

Three days later, during my mother's surgery, the surgeon came out to inform our family that there was no trace of the grapefruit-sized tumor, to his great surprise. However, he found cancer-positive lymph nodes, which were removed. Today, my mother and I say that we witnessed a miracle! This miracle deepened my thirst for knowledge. After my mother recovered, we often contemplated this miracle. Incidentally, she lived another 28 years and ultimately died from Alzheimer's as opposed to breast cancer.

About two years later, I told her that a cardiologist at Columbia University, Dr. Oz, was doing research on cardiac patients using a therapy called Reiki. He was finding at least a 50 percent faster healing rate for surgical patients who received Reiki contrasted to the control group who did not receive any therapy. We were intrigued! My mother and I signed up for the first level of Reiki. Believing that planet Earth was speeding up and in need of as many *Light*workers as possible, our instructor encouraged us to get all three certifications in one weekend, which we did. From my perspective, understanding, experience, and knowledge, I liken Reiki to references of how *Jesus* healed people.

One of the most vivid and cherished spiritual events of my life happened during my first attunement for Level 1 Reiki. As unbelievable as this may sound, *Jesus* appeared to me and handed me a rectangular, elaborately carved wooden box. He did not say anything, but he telepathically implied that he was passing his legacy on to me. I did not clearly see his face, but his presence was completely purposeful, loving, and matter of fact. It was abundantly clear:

> **I was to take his box of tools (knowledge) to use on my path. This was his box and he was entrusting it to me. I was to use the contents for the betterment of humanity.**

When one experiences a vision of this type, the mind's first response is denial or rejection. We ask ourselves, "Was that just my imagination? Was that real? Did that really just happen?" Yet, something inside me insisted that it was very, very real. While many other similar occurrences and synchronicities have happened during my life (too many to include here), this event stands out. My best description is that this vision sent ripples through my soul. It set me on the path which allowed me to awaken and *Snap Back* to the understanding and acceptance of my true nature.

In 2008, I took a 20-week Learning Strategies program called *Pathway to Enlightenment,* led by Jeddah Mali. As time progressed, her program was instrumental in explaining many of the *Divine* events that had occurred and continue to amplify in my life. Jeddah's program consisted of an explanation and a question-and-answer segment. The predominant component was a guided weekly meditation that experientially and gently guided us to our true self of *Being*, conscious of our own *Light*. Her program taught students to see how each and every one of us is the *Sea Of Awareness*, which is another name for *Source/God/The Divine*.

Jeddah offered a follow-up 12-week course, which I downloaded and studied voraciously. To this day, I still replay all of her profound recordings to further deepen my own understanding and connection. I also attended two years of small group mentoring with her in 2012 and 2013. Her teachings come from the *Brotherhood of Light*. They are truly some of the most profound teachings I've ever experienced. They helped me see with my inner eyes and hear with my inner ears rather than just with my five senses.

During many of Jeddah's meditations, I was guided into a state of *Being* which allowed me to surrender into *Unity Consciousness*. This state of *Being* is very difficult to explain to someone who has never experienced *It*. This is a truly *Bliss*ful, exquisitely beautiful state of *Being*. In this state, one merges completely with *The Divine* and experiences both Nothingness and Everythingness simultaneously. I have been there so many times that now my *Energy* field and human mind have been changed forever. It is my welcomed responsibility and privilege to pass this *Divine* knowledge on to you.

It is through all of these combined direct experiences that I have come to Trust this *Energy Source*. I have come to cherish my direct relationship with *Source/ God/The Divine*. In fact, I can say I have seen the face of *God*. I have seen *It* often, daily, almost 100 percent of my conscious non-sleep time. Because of this direct relationship and my surrender into *It*, I acknowledge I am *It*, and of course, I Trust *It*.

It is important to understand that this *Source*, this vast endless *Sea*, wants each of us to see *It*, to know *It*, to know that we are *It*, and to Trust *It*. It is said that when our *Light* shines so bright, it is our turn to shine our *Light* so that others may see their own *Light*, their own Beauty, and Trust this *Source*. Once they do so, they no longer suffer. They are freed to see their own *Divine* truth and their own *Light*.

CHAPTER 3

How to Enter into the State of *Being* of *Divine Trust*

The definition of Trust is the firm belief in the reliability or truth or strength of a thing, in this case, *God*. It is unquestioning. Trust is both a verb—the act of Trusting—and a noun—the state of being in Trust, which I call *Divine Trust*. When in this state, you feel cared for, you feel held, you feel Safe, you feel *Its* gentle Power, you feel *Its* Benevolence, and you feel *Its* Aliveness. You come to know *It* is absolutely reliable and is always there, waiting to be seen, felt, known, and experienced. The quickest way I have found to enter this state of *Divine Trust* is as follows:

STEP 1

- Sit quietly or lie down with your eyes closed.
- Follow your breath and imagine it is moving clockwise in a circle.

- With each inhale, visualize it moving from the bottom of the circle up the left side towards the top.
- With each exhale, visualize it moving from the top of the circle down the right side towards the bottom.

Important note: the only way to know *Source* is in the *Present Moment*. It is the doorway you must go through to reach the *Divine*. When you give your mind an assignment, such as following the breath, the mind's attention is taken up by that assignment. If your mind is consumed with the past or anxious about the future, you are not in the *Present Moment*. With practice, this gets easier. (See *Advanced Practice*.)

STEP 2

- Make an intention to see or feel *Source*. What you intend must manifest. This is a Universal Law. Please note: if you intend to be gentle, generous, kind, warm, benevolent, and accepting, you will be greeting *Source* with many of *Its* own innate characteristics.
- Open your heart, and be willing to experience something new.
- Keep your awareness open for bodily sensations. You might experience one or more of the following:
  - Expansion, or your energy moving outward or lifting upward.

- Feeling lighter, or even that you can no longer feel your body. You might not be able to feel where your body ends.
- A sensation that you are merging with this *Energy*.
- Awareness of warmth or tingling.
- Seeing *Light* swirling in different patterns or colors.
- You might perceive a warm soothing Peace come over you.

If you can be in a state of allowing, rather than *trying*, or expecting a certain outcome, you will experience more. Sometimes, the sensations may be so subtle that you may discount them. If you are trying too hard, you are telling the *Sea of Awareness* that it is difficult to sense these sensations, so that is what is manifested—difficulty and no sensations registered. Just relax, allow, and Trust that you *can* experience new things.

STEP 3

- Once you connect to *Source* in this way, you will experience a shift.
- You will be aware that you are noticing and experiencing an *Energy*.
- *It* is sentient and so *It* wants *you* to see *It*.

- The first couple of times I saw *It*, I heard an actual celestial celebration. I could hear applause and celebrations from a cheering chorus! I have come to embrace my psychic abilities.

- One of the first times I was aware that I was experiencing *Source*, I saw that *Energy* before me, but not actually in me. As I spent more time embracing this *Energy*, *It* started showing me more. Over time, as I surrendered to *Source*, I could feel and sense that *It* was also *in* me.

- The more you commune with *It*, the more you see, the more you experience, and the more you grow to Trust *It*.

- Continue to pay attention to the sensations your body is experiencing. Do you feel expansive or contractive? Do you see *Light* or colors? Do you hear anything?

STEP 4

- Make an intention to surrender to this *Energy*. Once you surrender to *It*, and call *It* into your body and the *Energy* field that surrounds your body, then you will feel sensations of expansion. This expansion feels like your body is becoming lighter and your *Energy* is moving outward. You can also feel, see, know, or sense *Light,* as in luminary *Light.*

- Let your body and *Energy* field merge with *Source.*

- When you surrender to *Source,* you can tangibly feel Safety, Security, *Bliss,* and the sensation of being gently held.

- Your perspective on any situation you bring to this *Energy* will instantly be transmuted by the *Light.*

- You will experience from this *Source Of Energy* the following:

  - Anything the mind labels negative is actually there to create a **Snap Back** moment. This includes anything your mind labels as "bad," "tragic", a "problem", or "something lacking", "missing", or "wrong".

  - Please note: the current way most humans operate is to label the event or situation as "bad" and endlessly repeat it in their mind, causing needless suffering and living in the past and/or fear of experiencing similar events in the future.

  - This benevolent *Energy* allows us to create the so-called problem as an opportunity to wake ourselves up. But rest assured: this event, whatever it is, is serving the *Light.*

- This is Trust!

> From this point forward, your life will be forever changed.

STEP 5

- Own that you are *This*.
- Say to yourself:
  - "**I AM** *This*."
  - "**I AM** *The Light*."
  - "**I AM** *Love*."
  - "**I AM** *Bliss*."
- Sit in *This*.
  - Let *It* perfuse not only your physical body, but also your *Energy* field, which is a sphere of *Light* about 6 feet around your body.
  - Note: The words 'I AM' are the two most powerful words in existence. Their power comes from 'I', meaning your consciousness, aware and in the *Present Moment*, and 'AM', meaning the *Divine*. Together, they create manifestation for whatever is attached to them. 'I AM'= *Source*.

STEP 6

- Summon a state of Gratitude.
- Give thanks that you are now awake. *You Are!*

     – You are Beautiful!

     – You are *Light*!

     – You are *Love*!

     – You are *Bliss*!

- Enjoy your *Being*!
- Realize you are *God*!
- Know you are *God*!
- Know you are *This*!

Now you are in the state of *Divine Trust*!

CHAPTER 4

The Advanced Method

*O*nce you can successfully perform Steps 1-6, you are ready to try an advanced method to connect to *Source*. At first, do it for about 10 minutes. Eventually, work up to 20 minutes.

STEP 1

- Prepare your environment.
- Silence your phone, computer, etc.
- Close your eyes.
- Let all thoughts of the day drop away.
- Let all thoughts of what you have to do drop away.
- Let all thoughts of your inbox and text messages drop away.

STEP 2

- Now, just sit or lie in the *Present Moment*. The *Present Moment* is the doorway to *All*.

- When your mind wanders, just bring it back to the vast Peace and Stillness of the *Present Moment*.
- Here, there is nothing to do except just *Be*.
- Watch yourself just *Being*.
- It is one of the most restful states there is.

To further explain, human *Beings*, as the expression of *God,* have the ability to become conscious—not just being awake, walking, and talking, but also being conscious of themselves as *Spirit* in the *Present Moment*. To be *aware* in the *Present Moment* is the *only* way that we can connect to *Awareness/God/Source*. Being conscious in the *Present Moment* gives us *all* the keys to the kingdom. All possibilities become available for us. When we are conscious and aware of our *Spirit* in the *Present Moment*, and we make the conscious effort to connect to *Awareness/Source,* *It* rushes right in and completely fills our entire body and *Energy* field with *Its Divine Essence* of perfection!

When we are conscious and in the *Present Moment*, and we see this *Energy* and *It* sees us, there is a magnetic pull. *Awareness* wants us to see *It,* and we want to see *Awareness*. From this point forward, *It* is always calling to us, and we are always calling to *It*. We each have an alluring magnetic pull towards one another. That is what is so beautiful about this experience: when we see each other, we see that we are really *One*: one and the same. It is like looking into a mirror.

Not only that, but every human *Being* is designed the same way. Every human *Being* can do this. Every human *Being* wants to do this. This magnetic pull is *the way home*. This is our calling. Up until this point, we have had amnesia. We have forgotten who we really are. As we remember from Chapter 1, this is by *Divine* design. We have forgotten of what we are made. When we have a sudden remembering, and we see the aliveness of *Source*, we experience a **Snap Back**.

For most people, this advanced technique can take some time to master. This is because we are trained to be controlled by our mind. When our mind does not have a job to do (i.e., watch the breath), it looks for something to do, something to ponder, something to solve, which is typically something negative. The mind separates. It looks for problems. It looks to protect itself. The mind most often controls our experience and does not let our *Being* rest, until we learn this knowledge.

When we are able to master this advanced method, it is a very profound experience. Once we are able to do this, just resting in the Stillness, we then have the best blank slate for intending or manifesting. We are in unmanifest territory— pure *Divine* energy—in the Stillness of the *Present Moment*. We can then intend to transform or create something, and go into the creation process. We literally move matter into creation by our intention, willingness, and our *God*-given ability to create. We are co-creators with the *Divine*. That's where magic truly happens!

CHAPTER 5

How to Reinforce *Divine Trust*

*T*he best way to reinforce the state of *Divine Trust* in *Source* is to sit in your own life's experiences. When we are resting in the Stillness of the *Present Moment*, as described in Chapter 4, we have a blank slate for surrendering to *Source* and releasing *any* situation into this vastness to be transformed. The process I use is as follows:

STEP 1

- Think of as many experiences as possible that have caused either you or others pain—whether they were physical, mental, or spiritual.

STEP 2

- Write these experiences down. Do not get too involved in each by letting it settle into your *Energy* field.

STEP 3

- Choose one of the least upsetting circumstances. Ask from *Source/God's* point of view, how could this event be good, or how does it serve the *Light*?
  - Rest assured that all events serve the *Light* and assist us in our evolutionary process forward to becoming more like our *Source*.
  - Sometimes, the event or situation might be serving to show us we have taken a wrong turn. But don't worry, we all will get there eventually! Once you commune with *Source* enough, you will sense this or know this and come to Trust this truth.

STEP 4

- Progress through your list until you see how all these events that you labeled "bad" turned out to be a blessing.
  - They are serving your own evolutionary process, or the evolutionary process of the human race.
  - Often, the most challenging times turn into the biggest blessings of our life.
  - They are powerful pivotal points that change our course and direct us along our path, which is perfect for our soul's growth.

- – It is looking back in hindsight that teaches us this truth.

- Once we can master the knowledge laid out in this book, we can skip this step, and start living from the flow of Life, in the state of *Divine Trust*, knowing that it is unfolding perfectly.

CHAPTER 6

How to Work With *Divine Trust* to End Suffering

*O*nce you have gotten this far into this process, you are now ready for the next step of your evolution.

- Think about your list from the last exercise and how, from *God's* perspective, *everything* serves the *Light*. Therefore, *nothing "bad" ever happens!*

- Sit in this truth.

- Trust this truth.

- *This is the end of suffering!*

If you are not able to do this with all events you labeled as a tragedy, be kind to yourself, and with time and practice, you will be able to see this truth! When I was first working with Jeddah, I found this concept difficult to grasp. I asked her, "How did Hitler serve the

Light?" Her answer to me was that *nothing*, not even a hair, is ever out of place according to the *Creator*. The design of everything is towards expansion and evolution. So even the darkness is serving the *Light*. At first, I could not comprehend this truth. It was only by immersion into *Source* and with my own maturation that I came to know this for myself.

It actually took me two years to be able to do this after the birth of my special-needs daughter in 1999. At that time, I had yet to experience this steadfast assurance and union with *Source*. Had I known this information before my daughter was born, I would have processed through this situation more quickly. Instead, I suffered for years. However, after I had practiced these processes for some time, it only took me about one week to fully process the Marjory Stoneman Douglas High School Shootings in 2018 (as you will see later on).

CHAPTER 7

How to Work With *Divine Trust* to Move into Happiness

*O*ften times, when I sit in the truth of our *Being-ness* and see my responsibility and relationship of co-partnering with this *Sea Of Awareness*, I am often consumed by a complete and utter *Bliss*! This state of *Being* makes my body and *Energy* field vibrate at such a high frequency that I feel this *Light* exudes out of every pore—and even my eyes. Many, including myself, have witnessed my eye color visibly change as this *Energy* seems to pour out of my eyes! To explain this state in words is not possible, but it is truly an exalted state. It goes beyond happiness into complete and utter *Bliss*. You feel completely perfect, just as you are, without having to do anything at all. In fact, *everything* is perfect and beautiful just as it is. Even those things that your mind would label as not yet perfect are (in this state) perfectly imperfect.

> **This state ushers in what would be considered complete Peace and Happiness.**

So, how do you get there? As you continue practicing the exercises in this book, you will gain more experience and more understanding. Your confidence in your *Divine* abilities will deepen. Your mind's control over your thoughts will lessen. You will spend more time being awake in the *Present Moment*. Eventually, you will embody *Divine Trust*. You will be able to reliably create from your *Divine* Soul. You will become transformed as you are not pushing or trying to control your outer environment. You become more allowing. You are living in the flow of life!

CHAPTER 8

How to Move out of Fear and into Peace and Safety

What I offer here is a bridge from where you are right now to a new way of experiencing and allowing the *Sea of Awareness* to dissolve your suffering. To leave the past experiences behind, you need a bridge. Being conscious in the *Present Moment* is the bridge.

Let's take the following example. A traumatic event such as a car accident or a violent crime occurs. When your mind looks at the event, it typically labels it as "bad". This is a form of resistance. Remember, the mind's main job is to protect. Sometimes, the mind resists that the event even happened. You may hear people say, "I can't believe this happened!" If the mind judges the event or situation as "bad," or that there is something missing, lacking, or wrong, it will tend to repeat these events in the mind's eye, causing suffering. This can go on for years or even decades. You are also stuck in the energy of the event just as if it is continuing to happen right now. You stay frozen, living in the past or in fear of it happening again in the future.

Fortunately, you can flip this negative state of mind around and gain back control just by shifting your perspective. When you say,

> **"Yes, this did happen, and yet, I am here and alive right now, and I am okay in this moment. I accept that it happened."**

This causes your mind to stop spinning and allows it to become quiet. Now you can shift back into the *Present Moment*. You can breathe. Also, you are saying to the *Sea of Awareness* that everything is fine. This enables your consciousness to gently shift out of the control your mind has had over you and into the *Present Moment*. On an energetic level, your *Being* goes from the vibration of not being Safe to being perfectly Safe and in Harmony. And magically, your entire vibration changes and thus, your *Present Moment* reality changes.

To be clear, I am not asking you to justify any event or condone violent actions. But once you say "Yes" to the event, you can clear the energy/emotional charge that has kept you trapped in the past. Once your vibration changes from this shift in perspective, you will begin to call more things of this higher vibration into your life.

You will now attract more like thoughts of Safety and more events that show you that you are Safe. This is how you build a bridge from a lower vibration or thought process to a higher vibration or thought process.

Having a bridge to a different experience brings Hope. The bridge is the *Present Moment* which allows a much needed rest from the mind endlessly repeating the past trauma or event, ushering in a new way of experiencing life. The *Sea of Awareness* interprets your new state of *Being* as one of Peace. In this new state, your pain and suffering has dissolved.

Let's explore an example that illustrates this concept. Two weeks after the 9/11 attack, I went on a spiritual retreat to learn the Sedona Method, hosted by Hale Dwoskin. One of the participants was a survivor. He had witnessed people jumping out of the Twin Towers. He also had to hide in a door frame of a local store to escape the tsunami of debris as the buildings collapsed. He narrowly made it out alive. All of his coworkers lost their lives. He was late to work that day, which by the grace of *God* allowed him to survive. But his mind could not let him rest. It hijacked his complete train of thought so that the events of 9/11 were all he could think about. And he suffered.

The Sedona Method is very similar to the some of the processes I present in *Divine Trust*. Both of these methods are meant to quiet the mind. Throughout the week, Hale gently worked with this participant in front of the entire group to lead him through a process to alleviate his mind from gripping his every thought. The goal was to arrive at Peace in the *Present Moment,* much as the way I explained above. In the *Present Moment,* everything is okay. You are in a place of Peace and Safety right now. By the end of the retreat, this man was openly more at Peace.

The ultimate goal of human evolution is to navigate every moment of your life with your mind aligned with *Pure Consciousness* so that you can live from your *Divinity.* Presently, human beings navigate from their mind controlling their everyday life, in survival mode. This is what is referred to as the "fight or flight" response. Physiologically, this triggers the reptilian part of the brain and its correlated sympathetic autonomic nervous system, flooding the body with a whole host of neurotransmitters and chemicals that are meant to function only for a short term.

When the body responds in this way for an extended period of time, there is a deleterious effect on the entire body. There is also a blockage of our natural ability to think clearly. When the mind is navigating our experience in this way, it holds us down and prevents us from being all that we can be, blocking our evolution. The mind is actually a *Divine* tool, but the way we have been trained to use it has been very negative and limiting. However, when your mind is cooperative and aligned with higher states of *Consciousness,* it becomes a supportive tool, the *Divine* tool the *Creator* meant it to be.

We are now on the brink of the promise of human evolution, and those reading this are part of this evolution. We are moving out of navigating from the everyday mind and moving into wholeness—the whole alignment of our body, mind, and *Spirit*. When we navigate from this aligned *Consciousness*, we take a quantum leap into living life as *Divine* beings, the highest expression of human potential.

Although the process I teach here to move us out of fear and into Peace and Safety may seem very contradictory, it works on *all* difficult events and situations. This was taught to me at the very beginning of Jeddah's teachings. She not only explained this process, but led us into the firsthand knowledge of experiencing it directly. I will guide you through this process so that you, too, can experience Peace and Safety.

First, I will explain the state of *Being* you need to be in to start the process, and then I will explain how and why it works.

STEP 1

- Sit quietly and breathe.
    - Follow the breath as was previously explained (see Chapter 3, How to Enter into the state of *Being* of *Divine Trust*).

STEP 2

- Say to yourself (whatever the event or situation), "It is okay just as it is."

STEP 3

- Tell the *Sea Of Awareness* that you *accept* the event or situation.

  – You accept that it happened, and you are still here alive and okay in this moment.

STEP 4

- Invite it (the event or situation) in without letting the event stick to your emotions or without feeling the initial sensation, i.e., hold it lightly.

  – Bring this event into the state of open acceptance and say 'Yes!' to the situation/opportunity: "Either I or someone else brought this into being; so it must be okay. I can look at it and accept it and understand that all things serve the *Light*."

Once you are able to welcome this situation/opportunity, this is the *Energy* you are putting out into the *Sea Of Awareness*. This is the instruction you are giving *It*. You are telling the *Sea Of Awareness* that whatever happened was meant to evolve you and all of creation. Then, the *Sea Of Awareness* must and will oblige your instruction by transforming or dissolving the charge that the event has on you, and you will feel held in Love and Safety. Of course, the assumption is that you have matured spiritually enough to sit still in the truth of your *Being*.

> **It is through open acceptance of the event or situation that completely transmutes your fear and moves you into the state of Safety!**

Please note that every practice and technique in this book is meant to be experienced in the *Present Moment*. If you are not able to feel Safe after practicing this technique, you might need to be guided into this state by someone who is experienced. Eventually, you will be able to experience and *know* that *everything* is perfect just the way it is, and that you are Held, Safe, and Perfect!

CHAPTER 9

Suffering Pushes You to Find
Your Way Out

*B*efore I had this knowledge and experience, I suffered! In 1999, after trying to conceive for five years, I became pregnant out of the blue. Looking back, the only shadow over my pregnancy was that I had consumed wine not yet knowing I was pregnant. In fact, I had met one of my best friends in California for a week-long tour of the wineries. Once I found out I was pregnant, I admit I was concerned that I had consumed too much wine early in my pregnancy. This added to the subtle fear I already had that my family history could also contribute to a birth defect; I had a severely mentally disabled older brother. My parents were never able to determine the origin of my brother's disability.

My mind played all kinds of nasty tricks on me. I had amniocentesis which checks for the possibility of certain genetic issues such as Down Syndrome, but not all genetic abnormalities. The results showed that my baby did not have Down Syndrome. The day my daughter was born, the most experienced doctor in the pediatric practice I was using came to the hospital to do a routine well-baby check. He took a one-second look at my daughter and told me that she had a *syndrome*. Of course, he was right. Through the medical advancement of mapping the human genome, it was determined that she had a genetic abnormality.

The next two years were spent figuring out exactly what her issues were and doing whatever I could to help her so that she would have the best possible outcome. For those two years, I would have described my state of *Being* as *depressed*. I was consumed by guilt for letting my guard down and going wine tasting during the most critical time of fetal development, even though I didn't know I was pregnant. I also blamed myself for creating this situation and making an innocent being suffer for my carelessness. In other words, I took complete responsibility for my daughter's condition. I beat myself up for what I perceived as my mistake.

My mind was spinning all the time. My feelings of guilt were amplified by the fact that while in college, I had been exposed to many compounds in the laboratories where I did research that could have also caused genetic mutations in my reproductive organs. Can you see how I made myself suffer? But because of this, to alleviate my own suffering, I had extra incentive to master this knowledge.

> You have to suffer before finding the way out. Suffering pushes you to look for relief from your pain. Once you find relief, you want to help others find their way out of pain and suffering, too!

Now, looking back, and with all my experience, I see how having a special-needs daughter actually assisted me in a multitude of ways. She made me a better person and a better orthodontist. She taught me behavioral management skills for the anxious patient. At the time of my daughter's birth, I worked in a large pediatric/orthodontist office where none of the doctors had the patience to deal with fidgety, apprehensive young seven-year-olds. They sent them all to me. Living with a special-needs child and learning how to manage her heightened fear and sensory issues made me a master of working with young patients. Because of the lessons my daughter taught me, I was able to put even the most fearful young patient at ease. So, *all* was a blessing.

Had I known then what I know now, I would not have suffered through two years of depression and guilt!

CHAPTER 10

The Grace of *Divine Trust*

*A*fter I gained this knowledge and experience, I had some very profound situations where I was able to apply *Divine Trust*. The events that occurred would be considered such big core wounds that they would pull almost everyone down. I will attempt to relay them here.

On January 25, 2018, my mother made her transition to the other side. She had Alzheimer's Disease. Her decline was rather slow and took about seven years. So, when the end came, I was able to spend every second by her side and practiced Reiki on her for hours on end. I practiced *Divine Trust* in the *Sea Of Awareness/Source* to see that she chose her path. Maybe Alzheimer's was her way of pulling away from me and the rest of our family to make this transition easier on all of us. Through holding a state of *Divine Trust*, I could see that this was exactly what was meant to be.

I was with her when she took her last breath. It was exquisitely beautiful, sad, and profound all at the same time. I can't imagine how I could have processed this without *Divine Trust*! We held her Catholic Mass for her Transition Ceremony on February 9, 2018.

I barely had time to process this when one of the biggest, most heart-breaking events of our time occurred. It was Wednesday, February 14, 2018. I was a practicing orthodontist for twenty-eight years in Coral Springs, Florida. One of my biggest referral schools was Marjory Stoneman Douglas High School, which was about one-and-a-half miles away.

I will never forget working on a patient that afternoon when one of the patients' mothers received an alert on her phone. In horror, she exclaimed that there was an active shooter at Douglas High School. We heard hours of sirens. A member of my staff could not reach her sister, who was a freshman at Douglas High School. In disbelief and total numbness, unable to continue, we ended the work day early. As I drove home, I saw twenty to thirty cars on all sides of the street. Parents, desperately trying to get to the High School, had created gridlock. Trying to make sure their teenagers were okay, they had abandoned their cars to walk the rest of the way. I can only imagine their panic.

That night, very little information was televised on the news. Some of my staff stayed up all night supporting those in need. Around 5 a.m., I got a call that our staff member's sister was among the seventeen teens who lost their lives. Later that same morning, we found out through social media that another one of the seventeen was one of our treasured patients. Due to complete shock, I canceled the rest of the week of seeing patients so that we could attend candlelight vigils and funerals. The community was beyond shock and beyond grieving!

The morning of February 15 was a blur. Numb with grief and pain, my office manager, head assistant, and I convened at the office. We were there to be of service, support, or help to anyone in need. When I got confirmation that one of my patients lost her life, an all-consuming feeling of compassion for her mother came over me. I had to console her. I bought a sympathy card and the most gorgeous orchid arrangement I could find, and jumped into my car to go see her.

Something was guiding me and urging me to be there for this mother. I knocked on her door, not expecting her to answer. When she did, I just grabbed her and hugged her, trying to take away some of her pain. I felt compelled to do … I don't know what. Maybe, somehow, to let her know that I was there with her, along with the entire world, trying to bear some of her load. We both *sobbed and sobbed.*

The following week was spent going to funerals and consoling parents, patients, staff, and myself. I was in shock, deep grief, and felt numb. Psychologists know that after such an event, people may suffer from

Post-Traumatic Stress Disorder, Survivor's Guilt, and Pathological Fear and Anxiety from not feeling Safe. This was a horrific event. The more I learned of the event, the worse I felt. I knew I had to gain control of these feelings.

My grief from both my mother's passing and the Douglas High School shooting lasted for less than a week, when I went deep into meditation with *Source/ God*. From this vantage point, and my Trust in *Its* benevolence, I was able to see the events from a higher, different perspective. *All* events serve the *Light*. So, I asked, "If this is so, then what is the purpose of this event; and, *how* does it serve the *Light*?"

The answer that came back is difficult to relay in words and on paper, but it translates into something like this:

> In order for humans to evolve, sometimes there has to be pain to bring about change. Pain often asks us to look deeply at ourselves and/or society. By doing so, we can see where we went wrong, where we went off track, and where we acted from hate rather than from *Love*.

> We as humans have freewill. We can use it to do good, or we can use it to do bad. When we use it to do things from a place other than *Love*, it is a sure sign that we are not connected to *Source*. It is also a sure sign that we have temporarily lost our way.

Some souls involved in the event may be
perceived as innocent souls and some as evil
souls. It is important to know that before they
incarnated, *all* souls made their decision to
play their roles for the purpose of evolving
themselves and the human race.

Knowing the above information partially helps
relieve the pain. Yet, it is by going into a state of *Divine
Trust*, and holding steadfast in this state, that allows us
to eliminate suffering. When we come to know *God/
Source* directly, we Trust that no life is wasted; no life is
lost in vain.

My understanding has grown such that I know that my
mother chose the time and the way she would leave the
physical world and so did the Douglas High School teens.
If that was so, can you imagine what brave souls all of those
Douglas High School kids were? They chose to incarnate
and then leave the physical world relatively young so
that they might change the world! When I look at this
event from this perspective, all seventeen kids are *heroes*!
Furthermore, the students and their families that lived
through it are all heroes, too! Everyone who realizes these
truths has the potential to be an instrument of change. This
allows us to learn how we each can be more responsible for
our own lives and teaches us how to be more *Loving*.

As the next two years unfolded, I would often go
to Pine Trails Park (the site of the candlelight vigils) in

Parkland on my lunch hour and just sit and give Reiki to the entire city. While doing this, I would see my visual field start to shimmer and adjust to this *Love* flowing through my hands!

Another principle that may add to the understanding of this specific event which occurred at Douglas High School is that generally, the more shocking or profound the core wound, the bigger/stronger the spirit is that chose this core wound! Can you imagine if all those affected by this event would come to understand the working model of existence and come to Trust *It*? They would have such a huge **Snap Back** to their original *Essence*, knowing, without a doubt, that they are *Presence*. This is the very purpose of incarnating, so that *God* can know *Its* magnificence! The entire city could be enlightened! If they could retain this knowledge of being home, this would end suffering and assist *the evolution of mankind*!

> **This is their Purpose! Now they can Awaken! Now they can be Free!**

I often sit in the truth that *God/Source* put me in the exact right place, at the exact right time, with the exact right knowledge to help ease all the suffering. Now all I need is the courage and the willingness to teach *It* and for those affected by the event to embrace *It*!

CHAPTER 11

Divine Trust Takes Me Home

W hat happened next seems unrelated, but whether or not that is true remains to be seen. I started having back pain in 2018 while leaning over my mother's hospital bed for one month. This was the beginning of my discovery that I had 17 bulging and 4 herniated discs which caused so much pain. Every day that I worked, bending over my patients, was damaging my body further. It became detrimental to my health to continue practicing orthodontics. Realizing this, I sold my practice at the end of August, 2020.

I planned a one-month spiritual retreat at an ocean-front condominium near my father. I was hoping to give my back a break and hang out with my dad. Six days into the retreat, my father became very sick. My thoughts were that, once again, *Divine* intervention had placed me at the exact right place at the exact right time! My father and I were able to share some of the best quality time of our lives before he passed over. My practice sold at the exact right moment. This perfect timing of my 'retreat' was *Divinely* orchestrated, at the exact right month, resulting in the time to devote to my father. Importantly, I now have time to share my knowledge of how Trusting *Light/Source* ends suffering!

In addition, if it hadn't been for my back issues forcing me to sell my practice, I would never have been inspired to write this book, nor would I have had the time. The day I started writing this book was December 9, 2020, the same day my father made his transition. It was a sudden decline of a ninety-three-year-old gentle man. It is precisely times like this that calling in a state of *Divine Trust* makes the biggest difference! It is completely different to think of *Divine Trust*—because you still suffer—but *while in a complete state of Divine Trust, nothing bad can ever happen*! Although I am still sad, this state of *Divine Trust* acts like a balm soothing any remnants of pain.

Just saying "nothing bad ever happens" helps start the state that leads me home. Once I connect to this *Bigger Than Me* state, I can see the bigger picture and how everything is taken care of by *Source*. It is almost as if something is smoothing or soothing away the pain.

My spiritual retreat was turned into an end-of-life caregiving for my father, which I shared with my sister. Once again, this state of *Divine Trust* assisted me through what initially (to the mind) might look like an evil twist of fate. Actually, all the synchronistic events led me to be in the exact right place at the exact right time. I am incredibly grateful!

CHAPTER 12

Bringing Heaven to Us

*T*he *end of suffering* has at least two components.

First, you need to hear, or learn, and experience this information. Sitting in a state of *Divine Trust always takes me home*, every time.

Second, you must take responsibility for your own state of *Being*.

I know that this knowledge and the state of *Divine Trust* helps, as I have worked one-on-one with many people to assist them into their own **Snap Back**. By teaching them how to use a state of *Divine Trust*, they ease out of suffering. However, there are those who don't really want to change, or who are too deeply attached to their own story and their own suffering.

The grace of *Divine Trust* has become my obligation to share with all of humanity. This knowledge is a welcome responsibility. If you don't experience *It*, you aren't living the life you are meant to live. Once you surrender to *Divine Trust*, your life takes on a whole new and enriched level of living. It is almost like moving from living in black and white to living in rich, vibrant technicolor! We are actually *bringing Heaven to us*! If you are ready and willing to embrace this knowledge, you will end suffering! Will you join me? Are you ready? If so, read this book again, and put the exercises into practice. Enjoy your newfound Peace and *Bliss*!

About the Author

Dr. Nancy Wiley received her B.A. in Biology from University of Maryland, Baltimore County. She then went on to receive her M.S. in Nutrition, and her D.D.S. and a Certificate of Orthodontics from Columbia University. She also received her Diplomat to the American Board of Orthodontics and Qualified Orofacial Myology Certification. She has done research at the Biology Department of UMBC and Columbia University as well as Johns Hopkins Medical School. She has published multiple scientific research papers.

After graduating from Columbia's Orthodontic Residency Program, Dr. Wiley moved to South Florida where she practiced clinical orthodontics in private practice for over twenty-seven years.

Dr. Wiley has practiced various forms of meditation for forty-three years. These have included Transcendental Meditation, Holosync (brain wave entrainment), and guided meditations with many teachers, including Jeddah Mali. She is a Reiki Master and practices many forms of energy medicine, some of which include EFT (Tapping), Spring Forest Qigong, and Diamond Feng Shui. She has taken many other courses that allow and foster the development of the right side of the brain, such as PhotoReading. She has had many mystical experiences that have allowed her to see beyond the veil. Having a regular meditation practice for four-plus decades, she has gained knowledge, experience, and skill in navigating the inner world. Because of this, she is dedicated to igniting a massive shift in human consciousness.

Connect with Dr Nancy at TrustTheDivine.com.

Acknowledgments

I would like to take this opportunity to extend appreciation and gratitude to all of the thousands of teachers whose books or lectures have inspired me, the most prominent being Jeddah Mali and her teachers, *The Brotherhood of Light*. I was first introduced to her by Pete Bissonette and Paul Scheele at Learning Strategies.

Next, I must thank all my *Your Year of Miracles* (YOM) transformational leaders, without which I would never have had the support or encouragement to make the changes necessary to start living from my *Higher Self*! The founder, Marci Shimoff, is a constant source of inspiration. She is such a life force, sparking our belief in ourselves. Other YOM leaders that have profoundly influenced me include Debra Poneman (the co-founder of YOM and founder of *Yes to Success*), Dr. Sue Morter (author of *The Energy Codes* and teacher of *Central Channel Breathing*), and Lisa Garr (creator of the *Aware Show*, who constantly brings YOM new thought leaders and expanded ideas), all beloved by me! Each has gifted to me so many tools, teachings, and experiences that have layered one on top of the other so that I may create the life of my dreams.

I have constantly been uplifted and fed positive energy by my two YOM coaches, Suzanne Lawler and Meta Mehling. Each have gently infused me with such sparkling energy, that how could I not achieve something miraculous!

My dearest Miracle sisters, Mary Forehand, Dr. Rhea Haugseth, Julie Watkins, and Gina Robichaux, have given lift to my wings and have constantly encouraged me to soar! There is some sort of *Supernatural Force* that is created by the joining of hearts with the express intention of creating our hearts' desires.

My former YOM sisters, Sangeeta Soman, Holly Jaleski, Arlene Morris, and Audrey Frigstad, are still connected to me and assisting me with their life force! Our hearts are inextricably entwined.

Judi Miller, who is another YOM member, has given me much direction, as she is a new author herself, writing *Perfect*, a beautiful and inspiring story of her life's journey. Thank you for your direction.

Margaret M. Lynch's work of *Tapping into Wealth* is so much more than a program for abundance. It is much more about using EFT (Emotional Freedom Technique), or Tapping, to remove limiting beliefs that hold us back from stepping into our true selves. Margaret's work was pivotal in helping me break through my limiting beliefs to make the positive changes necessary to bring *Divine Trust* to you.

I am profoundly thankful to Mary Forehand who was the first editor of *Divine Trust,* who gave me such encouragement that it catapulted me forward in such a positive way.

I am also so grateful to my sister, Judy Finkell, for her editing skills and amazing support.

My final editor, Angela Valentine, sparked such a creative force in me that we were able to imbed into *Divine Trust* some sort of *Supernatural Energy* and information. I am deeply grateful for our synchronistic meeting during a PhotoReading course.

I would also like to thank my Publisher, Geoff Affleck, who effortlessly guided me through every step of the way of getting *Divine Trust* published.

Thank you also to videographer Ari Feldmiller at Ren Videos who has helped me with the companion guided meditations to enrich your experience of *Divine Trust* and assist you on your journey into a state of *Divine Trust*.

Steve Lillo, my website developer, brought my vision to life on the internet and was inspirational in getting *Divine Trust* into your hands.

My husband and partner for the last 27 years, Tom Wiley, patiently holds down the fort and encourages me to bring into *Being* what I must. Because of you in my life, I have achieved more than I ever thought possible. And because of you and the love we share, I am able to stay grounded, even though I am often in altered states of *Being*. You know that I am here to change the world, and I profoundly appreciate your support.

Whitney Wiley, my beautiful, funny daughter has taught me so much and has brought out of me the best and the worst. You inspired me to find my True Self.

Loving thanks to Eleanor Gnizak, my mother and companion on my seeker's journey. Although you are no longer on this plane, I still know and feel you are with me. You have inspired me to become many things in life, and I know you are so very proud now of where our journey has taken me. I also feel your presence when I am writing, and I sometimes still hear your voice gently correcting my grammar. I also thank Raymond Gnizak, my father, for inspiring me in his own gentle way. I would also like to extend my appreciation and gratitude to the entire Gnizak, Biro, and Wiley families. All have taught me so much and have been there to support me in many ways.

My own Guides and Teachers in the unseen plane have grown in their ability to communicate with me as I have opened and allowed them to disseminate knowledge and teachings directly through me.

But most importantly, I am so humbled and deeply grateful that *Divine Trust* and the *Divine Itself* have partnered with me. They have given me not only such a rich life experience, but also the confidence and courage to assimilate certain truths and to have a full blown experience of enlightenment. They have been there to constantly support me and have communicated the teachings that they wanted known at this time in human history.

CPSIA information can be obtained
at www.ICGtesting.com
Printed in the USA
LVHW100847300722
724783LV00021B/754